Roger Coote and Diana Bentley

The Middle Ages

Firefly

In the Middle Ages, life was very hard for ordinary people. Not many **peasants** owned land. Most of them had to work on the land belonging to their master.

Harvest time was very busy. The peasants in the fields had to cut all the corn and tie it into bundles called sheaves. Then the sheaves were loaded on to a cart and taken to be stored. If the crop was good everyone was happy because there would be enough food to eat during the winter.

Some peasants were called **serfs**. They belonged to their master and had to live in cottages near his fields. They were not allowed to move away from there. If a serf ran away, his master would send men to chase him and bring him back.

7

The monks in their **monasteries** led a quieter life than the peasants. The monk who was in charge of the monastery was called the abbot. The monks spent some of their time praying, and some working in the monastery.

In the Middle Ages, monks were almost the only people who knew how to read and write. Some monks spent many hours copying religious books and drawing illustrations for them. There was no other way to make books in those days, because printing had not been invented.

Sometimes there were arguments between one **noble** and another. If enemy soldiers came to attack, the peasants would leave their houses and shelter in the courtyard of the castle. Often the enemy soldiers would burn down their houses and take their crops.

When a nobleman was not fighting, he kept in training by going hunting. He and his men rode on horseback and practised with bows and arrows and spears. The peasants in the picture are gathering firewood.

15

Gradually more and more people left the countryside and went to live in towns. Some serfs went to escape from their masters. If they were not caught, they might ask the lord mayor of the town or an important noble to protect them.

In the middle of each town there was a market. It was a busy place. The **merchants** called out to get people to buy their goods, and the people tried to make the merchants sell their wares more cheaply. All sorts of everyday things were sold, such as food and pots and pans. There might also be expensive silk all the way from China. Some merchants sold beautiful wooden boxes, rare spices, and fine swords and daggers from Spain.

In those days, all the craftsmen who made a certain kind of goods belonged to the same club or **guild**. Shoemakers all belonged to the shoemakers' guild, and they all had their shops in the same street. Other types of craftsmen had their own guilds and their own streets.

In some old towns you can still see streets with names like Shoemakers Lane, Goldsmiths Row or Tanner Street. These names probably date from the Middle Ages.

Trade was very important in the Middle Ages. Some merchants bought and sold goods from nearby towns, and others traded with countries far away. Ships carried all kinds of cargo – wheat, oil, wine, woollen cloth, linen, silk, spices and ivory. Goods were also carried overland on the backs of mules.

In the great hall of a castle poets, jugglers, dancers and musicians sometimes came to perform for the nobles. **Knights** held jousting contests outside the castle. Two knights would ride towards each other on horseback. Each knight tried to knock the other one off his horse using the long lance he carried.

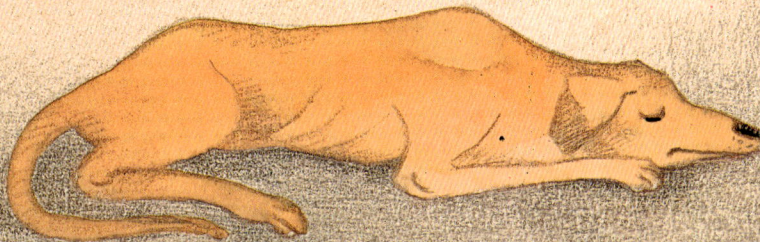

Laws were made by the king. If nobles or merchants or important **clergymen** wanted the king to make a new law they would ask to see him and tell him why. If the king agreed, the law would be passed. Someone might also tell the king if a law was being broken, and ask him to punish the **criminal**.

Important towns in the Middle Ages often had a large, beautiful **cathedral**. Each cathedral was designed by a master **mason**. He made sure that the builders did their job properly and followed the plan he had drawn of the cathedral. The cathedral was made from large pieces of stone, which were cut to the right size with a saw. Beautiful windows were made from coloured glass. The people of the town sometimes helped raise the money needed to build their cathedral. When it was finished, they would go there to pray.

Although the Middle Ages were hundreds of years ago, some of the things from that time have survived. The names of some towns and streets come from the Middle Ages, and some of the laws we have today are based on laws that were made then.

New words

Cathedral A very large church built in an important town

Clergymen Men of the Church, such as monks, parsons and bishops

Criminal Someone who breaks a law

Guild A group of craftsmen who all make the same goods

Knight A soldier who fought on horseback

Mason Someone who builds things with stone

Merchant A person who makes money by buying goods and selling them again at a higher price

Monastery A religious building where monks live and work

Noble An important person in the Middle Ages. Nobles often owned a lot of land and had many serfs. Some nobles had their own soldiers.

Peasant An ordinary person who worked on the land

Serf A peasant who belonged to his master

Trade Buying and selling goods for money or swapping them for other goods

Books to read

If you would like to find out more about the people who lived in Middle Ages, these books will help you.

The Everyday Life of a Cathedral Builder by Giovanni Caselli (Macdonald)
The Everyday Life of a Florentine Merchant by Giovanni Caselli (Macdonald)
Growing Up in the Middle Ages by P. Davies (Wayland)
How They Lived – A Medieval Monk by Nigel Hunter (Wayland)
How They Lived – A Medieval Serf by Stewart Ross (Wayland)
Living in Castle Times by R. Gee (Usborne)
Looking at a Castle by Brian Davison (Kingfisher)
The Middle Ages by Barry and Anne Steel (Wayland)
See Inside a Castle edited by R.J. Unstead (Kingfisher)